The Running Shoes

Story by Angelique Filleul

Illustrations by Sharyn Madder

Everyone at school was talking about
the cross-country races.
They were going to be held
the following week.

"I'm going to win our race!"
grinned Olivia.
"My new shoes will help me run
much faster than anyone else."

Alex looked down
at her old running shoes.
She wished she had
a new pair like Olivia's.

Olivia ran over to Alex.
"Do you like my new shoes?"
she asked.

"They look nice," said Alex.

Olivia looked down at Alex's shoes.
"You've had yours for a long time,
haven't you?"

"Yes," answered Alex,
suddenly wishing her old shoes
would disappear.

That afternoon, Alex talked to Mom
about the big race
while she helped her in the kitchen.
"We are having our cross-country race
next week," she said.

"That sounds exciting," said Mom.
"How do you think you will do?"

"I don't think I'll win," said Alex.
"Olivia will. She's got the best shoes.
But I'll try hard to finish.
It's a much longer race this year.
Will you and Dad come and watch me?"

"I'll be able to," said Mom.
"But your dad might be too busy
at work."

"I'd really like it if he could come,"
said Alex. "I always run faster
when both of you are watching."

During the weekend, Dad and Alex
went out for a run together.

"You are running very well, Alex,"
said Dad.
"You could win your race next week.
Just remember not to run too fast
at the beginning."

"Olivia keeps saying
she's going to win
because she's got new running shoes,"
said Alex.

"Some of the fastest runners in the world don't wear shoes at all," smiled Dad.

On the day of the cross-country races,
when Alex was just putting on
her running shoes,
Olivia ran over to her.

"My dad says the best runners
have the best shoes," grinned Olivia,
and she ran off to join the others.

Not long after that, the races began.
Alex saw Mom on the sideline
waving to her.
But she couldn't see her dad.

Soon it was time for Alex's race.

The children headed
across the hilly fields
toward the first flag.

Olivia was out in front,
and Alex thought about
catching up to her.
But then she remembered
what her dad had said.

She decided to stay
with most of the other children.
It was too soon
to try to take the lead.

She would wait for the right moment.

As she ran down the last hill,
Alex saw Mom
standing among the other parents.
Then she saw Dad!
He had come, after all!

Olivia was still in the lead
but she wasn't too far ahead.
Alex knew that this was the moment
to speed up.

She ran faster
than she had ever run before.
She tried so hard
that she ran past Olivia
and crossed the finish line first.

Mom and Dad rushed over to her.
"That was a great race!" cried Mom.

Dad smiled and said,
"Now, do you still think you need
a new pair of running shoes?"

"No," said Alex.
"I like these old ones.
They are the best running shoes!"